PRINCESS

COLORING BOOK

THIS BOOK BELONGS TO:

_____

Thank you.

We hope you enjoyed our book.

As a small family company, your feedback is very important to us

Please let us know how you like our book at:

 **oclaudeauthor@gmail.com**

 **oclaudeuauthor**

CPSIA information can be obtained
at www.ICGtesting.com
Printed in the USA
BVHW062126180521
607553BV00012B/1979